Fun with
Fabric

Fun with Fabric

Sew, cut, print and stick with retro and vintage fabric

COLLINS & BROWN

First published in the United Kingdom in 2013 by
Collins & Brown
10 Southcombe Street
London
W14 0RA

An imprint of Anova Books Company Ltd

ISBN 978-1-90844-990-0

A CIP catalogue record for this book is available from the British Library.

10 9 8 7 6 5 4 3 2 1

Photography by Alun Callender
Step illustrations by Kate Sutton

Reproduction by Mission Productions Ltd, Hong Kong
Printed and bound by 1010 Printing International Ltd, China

This book can be ordered direct from
the publisher at www.anovabooks.com

To my partner Jim and my daughter Polly

Contents

Introduction   6

PART 1
Vintage and
Retro Fabrics   10

My passion for textiles   12

Ever so simple   16
Box clever   18
Pretty pots   20
Shine a light   22
Sitting pretty   28
Edgy tea towels   32

Fabric pictures   34
My favourite fabrics   36
Framing fabric   38
Flower power   40

Patchwork   44
Patchwork throw   46
Strip patchwork   50

PART 2
Printing Fabric   54

The joys of printing   56

**Printing from masking-tape
and paper stencils**   58
Here's how!   60
Summer bunting   64
Sunshine and showers   66
Wall tidy   70
Geometric scarf   74

**Printing using an exposed
screen**   78
Here's how!   80
Christmas stocking   82
Table runner   86

Digitally printed fabric   90
Here's how!   92
Lavender bags   94
Floral cushion   96

Templates   102
Suppliers   110
Acknowledgements   111
Index   112

Introduction

Ever since I was a student in the late 1980s, I've been fascinated by 1950s style and design: I just love the bold, geometric shapes and vibrant colours of this period, whether it's in textiles, furniture or simple pieces of homeware. I've found myself particularly drawn to Scandinavian designs, especially those on ceramics. I love the Swedish designs of Stig Lindberg (for Gustavsberg) and Marianne Westman (for Rörstrand) and the illustrative patterns on some earlier pieces from the Finnish company Arabia and the Norwegian company Figgjo Flint. I also like 1960s Marimekko fabrics, with their eye-catching, extra-large patterns and bold, vivid colours.

I was a child in the 1970s and my parents sometimes shopped in Habitat. I particularly recall a bright green sofa they bought that had green chrome arms and also a bright plastic Crayonne ice bucket – and many of my favourite projects feature similarly strong and vibrant colours. My parents also bought a few pieces of Danish furniture from Heals, at a time when many other people favoured the pretty and more 'feminine' designs from Laura Ashley and Sanderson. I, too, have steered away from pastels, preferring the bold!

I live with my partner, Jim, who shares my passion for retro style, and our daughter, Polly, in a small town in the south-west of England, surrounded by beautiful countryside. Our house couldn't be more different to its surroundings. It's a modern, four-storey eco townhouse clad with wood. Our house started as a blank canvas and we have transformed it into a colourful, happy home.

I have an eye for an interesting bargain and can spot a piece of fabric that I love from a car boot full of junk, while Jim loves re-wiring retro lamps and helping me with restoration projects. Together, we breathe new life into old fabric, retro objects and furniture that we've found in a variety of places: at car boot sales, in second-hand shops, on eBay and at markets. We've never taken any notice of trends – we just choose to live surrounded by fabrics and items that we love.

My friends often say that they are inspired by the way in which we've decorated our home and they regularly ask me for tips on how they can achieve the same look in their own homes. In 2008 I decided to start a blog alongside my company website, which now has over 1,000 subscribers – so it seems that I'm not the only person who has fallen in love with this period and design style! This book brings together projects which you can easily incorporate into your own home and you can adapt the designs to suit whatever fabrics you can find – I will also show you some simple techniques for screen printing your own fabrics. The projects in this book range from ever-so-easy items that you can make in a matter of minutes, to bigger projects such as patchworks and table runners – but, as I'm a busy mum, I've concentrated on simple shortcuts that even the most novice stitcher can master.

I've had great fun devising these projects and drawing inspiration from my collection of vintage fabrics and my own illustrations. I hope my enthusiasm is infectious – now go and have fun with fabric!

1

Vintage and Retro Fabrics

My passion for textiles

It was during the late 1980s in Manchester that I spotted an eye-catching poster for an event called 'Design In The Fifties'. It was here that my love of 1950s design (especially textiles) began. I didn't have money to buy fabrics until years later, but the seeds had been planted – they just lay dormant for fifteen years!

In January 1997, I moved to Brighton and started sourcing and collecting vintage textiles. I bought only the fabrics I loved and I seemed initially to be attracted to geometric 1950s ones (avoiding chintzy rose designs!). In those days, I don't think many people realised that these fabrics would become collectables one day, so I often got them for bargain prices. I didn't know that these fabrics would later be popular, either – I was just buying them because I loved them.

I started finding more fabric during the early eBay days. By this stage I could often spot a rare textile by sight, as I'd done a lot of research. The fact that very few 1950s fabrics had a name printed on the selvedge was to my advantage, as people often didn't know what they were selling. The fabrics that I started collecting were often screen-print geometric 'atomic' designs, with just a few primary colours and designs similar to the work

of Miró, Kandinsky and Klee. My mum was a maths teacher and my dad a science teacher, so it's quite possible that their scientific influence was playing a small part here!

Later I began to collect fabrics from the 1960s and 70s with louder, often larger prints and more juvenile designs. I love op art 1960s screen-print patterns (similar to the work of Bridget Riley).

EBay is an invaluable source for finding a wide range of fabrics and has helped me to increase my collection.

Recently, the popularity of 1950s design has rocketed and now it's very difficult to find affordable examples of genuine 1950s textiles. Thankfully, many of the fabrics in my collection have recently been re-printed and produced by companies such as Sanderson and the Centre For Advanced Textiles in Glasgow – fabrics by Marian Mahler, Jacqueline Groag and Lucienne Day, to name a few. These good-quality fabrics are still quite expensive (and are sometimes screen printed), but many other fabric companies have produced their own more affordable 1950s-style retro fabrics digitally, appealing to quilters and crafters who want to buy just a fat quarter (50 x 56 cm/18 x 22 in.) of fabric.

Vintage fabrics need to be treasured – but also enjoyed. It's a great feeling to be able to re-use them in modern-day life. Not only is it good to recycle, but these fabrics are a wonderful addition to any home. I hope that what you see here will inspire you to fill your own home with fabulous textiles that you can enjoy every day.

Ever so simple

If, like me, you love fabric, you'll find it hard to throw away
even the tiniest scrap of a precious vintage or retro material
– your cupboards and drawers will be full to overflowing
with treasures that you just know you'll find a use for some day.
This chapter features some really quick and easy projects that
will enable you to showcase even the smallest pieces and give
them new life. They really couldn't be more simple to make:
if you can wield a glue stick and sew in a reasonably straight
line, you can create all of these in next to no time! If you
have kids, why not get them to help with projects like the
fabric-covered matchboxes (page 18) and pots (page 20)?
It's a fun way to spend an afternoon – and you'll be passing on
your passion for fabrics to the next generation!

Box clever

With a few chocolate coins or jelly beans inside, these little boxes make lovely gifts for Christmas stockings and party goody bags! They require no sewing, are quick and easy to create, and make a fun activity to do with your kids. This is also a great way of using up fabric scraps that are too small for other projects.

You will need

A variety of cotton fabrics (ones with a small design are best)

Empty matchboxes in a variety of sizes

White paper

Coloured paper

Glue stick

Sharp scissors

Why not...
Make a matching mini lavender bag to pop inside or have several boxes to store small items of jewellery in?

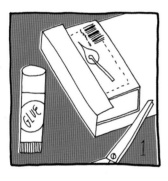  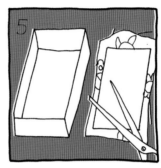 

1 Cut a piece of white paper slightly wider and longer than your matchbox. Apply glue to one side, then wrap the paper around the matchbox.

2 When the glue is dry, trim off any excess white paper. (The paper is to prevent the writing on the matchbox from showing through the fabric; it also helps to make the matchbox sturdier.)

3 Now do the same with a strip of fabric – although you needn't worry about the fabric joining together on the bottom of the box. When the glue is dry, trim off any excess fabric.

4 Cut out a rectangle of paper in a contrasting colour and glue it to the underside of the box.

5 Now cut a rectangle of paper exactly the same size as the bottom of the inside of the drawer. Cover it with glue, then cover the paper with fabric. Again, trim around the edge.

6 Finally, glue the fabric-covered rectangle to the inside of the drawer.

There you have it – a pretty fabric box ready to be filled with goodies!

Pretty pots

This is another easy project that requires no sewing. I came up with the idea while tidying the cardboard tubes that I use to post my screen prints in. I'm often left with odd-sized ends, so this makes good use of them! You can use the pots as storage for pens, knitting needles, or anything else that takes your fancy, or make them purely decorative, like the ones shown below – they look fabulous with just a few flowers or dried seed heads.

You will need

Strong cardboard posting tube
Sharp craft or utility knife
Cutting mat
Fabric
Sharp scissors
Glue stick
Plastic tube end

Why not...
Place an empty glass jar inside
the tube so that you can add water and
flowers and use it as a vase?

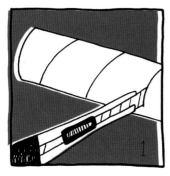

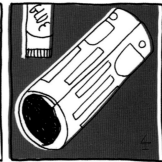

1 Decide how tall you want your pot to be. Using a sharp craft or utility knife on a cutting mat, carefully cut your tube to the desired length. (Don't worry too much if it's not perfectly straight – this is the edge that will be covered.)

2 Now cut a rectangle of fabric just slightly taller and wider than you need for the tube, making sure that the top edge is completely straight.

3 Fold one short end of the fabric over to the wrong side and glue. Now cover the whole piece of fabric in glue, including the folded-over end.

4 Wrap the fabric around the tube, making sure that the straight top edge is placed around the straightest end of the tube, level with the top, while the other end overlaps the base of the tube.

5 Fold the overlapping edge over to the inside of the pot and push in the white plastic tube end to form the base.

6 Now add whatever you want to keep in the pot!

Shine a light

We've sourced many retro and vintage lamp bases over the past years from car boot sales and it's great fun making lampshades in interesting fabrics to go with them. The beauty is that you can make new shades if you fancy a change and they're a fraction of what you would pay in the shops. Also, no one else in your street will have the same!

You will need

This project uses a flat-packed lampshade kit, which contains everything you need (apart from your chosen fabric) and precise instructions. You can buy these online in a variety of shapes and sizes.

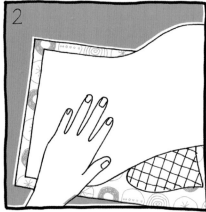

1 Place the long, self-adhesive panel from the kit on top of your fabric, making sure that the pattern on the fabric is straight and in line with the edges of the panel, and cut the fabric to about 2.5 cm (1 in.) larger all around than the lampshade panel.

2 Place the fabric right side down on your work surface, with the self-adhesive panel on top. When you're happy with the positioning, carefully peel back about 10 cm (4 in.) of the backing paper from the panel. Place the panel sticky side down on the fabric and smooth it out. Work down the whole length, smoothing the fabric out from the middle as you go.

Why not...
Make a matching
cushion?

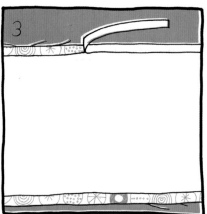

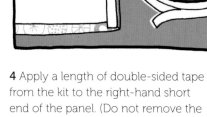

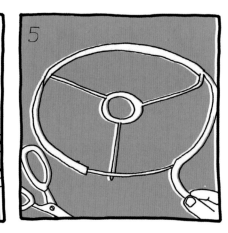

3 Cut off the surplus fabric level with the panel. Snap back the long edges of the panel until the hidden PVC strip along each edge breaks. Remove the PVC to leave the fabric covering.

4 Apply a length of double-sided tape from the kit to the right-hand short end of the panel. (Do not remove the backing from the tape at this stage.)

5 Stick double-sided tape along the edge of both lampshade rings, pressing it firmly around the wire. Remove the backing paper from the tape on both rings. (You might need to get an extra pair of hands to help at this stage, as it gets a bit sticky!)

Scandinavian sources...

I recommend sourcing your Scandinavian fabric from Hus and Hem, Northlight Design or The Swedish Fabric Company. These shops all specialize in Scandinavian design.

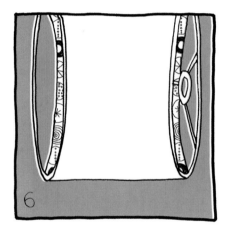

6 Starting at the left-hand end of the panel (the one without the double-sided tape), place the rings on opposite edges and slowly roll them around the panel.

7 When you get to the end, remove the backing paper from the double-sided tape that you applied in step 4 and press both ends of the panel together.

8 Fold over the surplus fabric covering all the way around, so that it covers the inside of the lampshade rings. Using the serrated edge of the plastic tool provided in the kit, carefully push the surplus fabric under the rings for a neat finish.

Now add to your favourite lamp base and enjoy!

Vintage or retro?

The words 'retro' and 'vintage' are often misused. Retro-style fabric is fabric that looks like an earlier one, whereas vintage fabric is fabric that dates from any time between the 1920s to twenty years before the present day.

Although it's getting more and more difficult to find genuine vintage fabrics, there are some fabulous retro-style designs around – so you can still make lovely soft furnishings that aren't available on the high street without breaking the bank. Check out the suppliers list on page 110. Just make sure that the fabric weight is suitable for the project you have in mind: for anything that's going to be subjected to a certain amount of wear and tear, it's generally better to use a furnishing-weight fabric. The cushions shown opposite are mostly made from vintage furnishing-weight fabric, with a modern plain white linen as the cushion back.

Don't be afraid to mix vintage and modern repro fabrics in the same piece. There are no hard-and-fast 'rules': if you like it, that's all that matters!

Sitting pretty

We picked up a couple of 1970s fibreglass stools from a local recycling centre, one of which had a horrid brown velvet pattern that reminded me of an old caravan interior. I knew the stools would look great covered in new fabric: all I needed to do was make what amounted to a couple of large shower caps!

You will need

Stool
Fabric
Pencil
Tape measure
Sewing machine
Approx. 1 m (40 in.) elastic,
15 mm (½ in.) wide
Clear adhesive tape

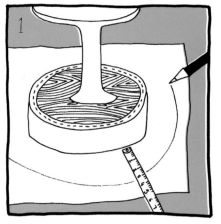

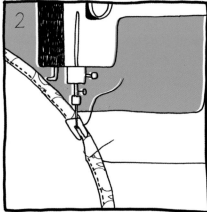

1 Place the stool upside down on your fabric about 12 cm (5 in.) from the edge. Taking a pencil and your tape measure, draw a line 10 cm (4 in.) from the base of the seat all the way around the fabric, thus creating a large pencil circle.

2 Cut out the fabric circle. Fold over 2 cm (¾ in.) to the wrong side and machine stitch all the way around, leaving a 4-cm (1½-in.) gap just before you reach the starting point.

Why not...
Make another cover in a different fabric, so you can alternate when one is in the wash?

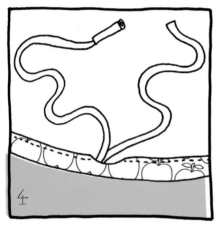

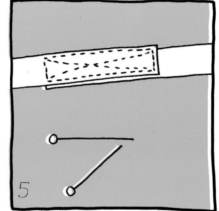

3 Wrap a length of elastic around the edge of the stool seat, stretching it slightly, and overlap the ends by about 4 cm (1½ in.). Cut to this length.

4 Wrap adhesive tape around one end of the elastic, so that it resembles the end of a shoe lace. Tuck the taped end of the elastic into the gap in the hem and thread it all the way through, making sure the other end of the elastic remains poking out.

5 Overlap the ends of the elastic by about 4 cm (1½ in.) and pin. Stitch across the ends in a box shape, then stitch diagonally across the box in cross to form a really strong join. Stretch the cover over the stool. If you wish, you can slipstitch the gap in the hem closed – but as it will be on the underside of the stool, it won't be seen.

Now you have your colourful retro stool cover!

Patterns and prints

The vintage fabrics that I love most tend to have big, bold patterns; combining several of them in the same piece can be slightly overwhelming, so always think about the scale of the patterns when you're using two or more fabrics together. Mix large prints with medium- or small-scale ones, or even with plain colours, so that they can stand out in all their glory.

Many of the fabrics I use have geometric or symmetrically arranged motifs, so it's particularly important to make sure that the motifs aren't skew-whiff on the finished item. Bear this in mind when you're cutting out and stitching or sticking.

On small items such as the covered boxes on page 18, make sure your fabric motifs are centred. You can do this by making a simple preview window: cut a section the same size as the front of your box out of the middle of a piece of card, place it over the motif to make sure it will fit, mark the fabric with a pencil or air-erasable marker pen, and then cut out. Patchworkers call this 'fussy cutting' – and I'm proud to be a fuss-pot!

Edgy tea towels

This project is so quick and simple that you can make it while the coffee is brewing! The apple fabric that I used came from Graziela (bygraziela.com) and is an original 1970s design that has been re-launched. The vintage flowery one in the photo was sourced on eBay: I love the bright orange, deep blue and purple colours within it. The green triangles fabric is a new linen design from Sweden.

You will need

Plain white cotton tea towel

Tape measure

Pins

Scissors

Sewing machine or hand-sewing needle

Matching thread

Why not...
Use the same technique to brighten up a plain hand towel or flannel?

1 Cut a straight panel of print fabric 1 cm (³⁄₈ in.) wider than the tea towel and roughly 16 cm (6¼ in.) deep. Fold all the edges over to the wrong side by about 5 mm (¼ in.) and press flat.

2 Pin the fabric to the bottom of the tea towel, leaving a narrow border of white showing along the bottom.

3 Sew by hand or with a machine and then press all over.

Fabric pictures

Vintage fabrics are to be enjoyed and treasured – and what better way to do this than to display them as pieces of art? Whether you choose to frame a piece in its entirety, so that you can see the original design in all its glory, or to cut out small sections and make a brand new picture, this chapter shows you how to create your very own fabric gallery.

We've gone for a very clean, crisp style of décor in our home, with painted white walls that show off our treasures and decorations to their very best. My picture frames follow the same pattern – they're mostly plain white. With a tin of emulsion paint and a small paintbrush, you can transform battered junk-shop finds into frames worthy of the trendiest gallery!

My favourite fabrics

I have been framing pieces of fabrics for years, as they make wonderful splashes of colour and are often pieces of art in their own right. Some rare pieces are far too good to cut up and deserve to be framed, admired and enjoyed. Here are some of my favourites, which I have around our home.

The geometric triangles fabric in the centre of the photo opposite dates from the 1950s and is called 'Pythagoras'. I went to Stockholm around eight years ago and fell in love with this fabric in a shop that was reproducing it for around £350 a metre. It's by Sven Markelius, a famous twentieth-century Swedish architect, and is a screen-print design on linen. Eighteen screens were used to produce it! I couldn't even afford half a meter, but last year I was fortunate enough to come across this piece of the original 1950s linen on eBay. I shall enjoy looking at it for years – and it's also a fond reminder of my trip to Stockholm.

The fabric on the left is an original 1950s spun rayon fabric designed by Marian Mahler, while the fabric on the far right is by Jacqueline Groag, a Czech designer; this one is really special to us, as Jim's parents used to have it in their living room.

Framing fabric

Most frame shops will frame fabric for you, but they will charge a lot. The good news is that it's really easy to do it yourself! Choose a simple frame that won't detract from the fabric. Car boot sales, garage sales and charity shops are good sources of inexpensive frames. If you're lucky, the window mount inside the frame will be in good condition, so you'll be able to re-use it, too – but if it's damaged, ready-made window mounts are available reasonably cheaply from home stores and art shops.

You will need

Frame
Fabric
Masking tape
Scissors

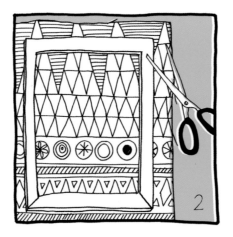

1 Start by ironing your fabric, so that it will lie nice and flat.

2 Lay the fabric on a large, flat surface and carefully place the window mount from the frame over the piece, so that you can see what will appear in the frame. If there is a large amount of excess fabric around the edge of the mount (and the fabric isn't too valuable), trim it with sharp scissors, leaving a few centimetres (an inch or two) overhanging.

3 Carefully turn the mount and fabric over and secure the fabric to the mount with a few small pieces of masking tape.

4 Place the mount and fabric right side down in the glass frame. Once you're happy with the positioning, you can remove the masking tape. Place the back of the frame (which is usually made of hardboard) on top. Carefully fold the fabric over the edges of the hardboard, making sure it isn't

4

puckered or creased, and tape it in place with masking tape.

5 Secure the hardboard back of the frame in place. If the fabric is valuable, remove the masking tape; if it isn't, you can leave the tape in place, although, over time, it will mark the fabric.

In the frame

It's very important to hang your framed fabric away from direct sunlight to prevent any fading and sun damage. Natural fibres such as cotton or silk are particularly at risk. And it's not just the colour: as the chemical bonds break down through exposure to ultraviolet light, the fabric itself can become brittle and prone to breakage.

It is possible to buy picture-framing glass that has been specially coated to provide UV protection, but this is an expensive option that's probably best reserved for really valuable, museum-quality pieces.

To minimize the risk of sun damage, swap your fabric pictures around regularly, and hang them in different parts of the house, so that they're exposed to differing amounts of UV light.

Flower power

I chose some 1960s and 70s floral fabrics for my picture of flowers in a striped vase (shown opposite, far right), as I was particularly drawn to the bold colours. The beauty of using ready-printed motifs is that you can create something really vibrant and colourful, even if you're not very good at drawing. If you do want to draw your own motifs, however, draw them on the paper side of the bonding web at the end of step 2.

You will need

Plain white fabric for the background
Colourful fabric (possibly scraps)
Green fabric for flower stalks and leaves
Fusible bonding web
Iron
Sharp scissors
Pencil
Frame (or piece of MDF or strong card)

1 Choose a square or rectangle of fabric for the background panel. (If you have a particular frame in mind, check that the background will fit into the window mount.)

2 Iron your fabric pieces so that they are nice and flat. Turn them over and place fusible bonding web on top, rough side down. Press with a warm iron to fuse the web to the fabric.

3 Cut out the flowers that you want to use, then cut some long stalks and leaves from plain green fabric.

4 Now for the fun part! Arrange your stalks and flowers on the background fabric. You might like to overlap some of the flowers or use smaller flower pieces for the middle of larger ones. Keep stepping back to look at your design, as viewing from further away can be helpful. You needn't worry about the vase at this stage.

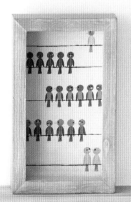

Other ideas...

If you don't want to hang your fabric picture on the wall, you could appliqué it to a bag, apron design or cushion.

5 When you're happy with your design, make a few light pencil marks on the background fabric to show you exactly where to re-position the pieces. Carefully remove the backing paper from the back of each flower and stalk piece, then replace it on the background. Using a warm iron, gently press each piece of the picture onto the background panel.

6 Make the vase in the same way – either from one piece of red-and-white striped fabric or from individual strips. Place a piece of cotton over the entire picture and press all over.

7 Frame your picture under glass (this is my preferred method, as the fabric will never get dusty!) or stretch it over an MDF board or a piece of strong cardboard and staple or tape it to the reverse.

Using fusible bonding web

Fusible bonding web takes the hard work out of appliqué, but there are a few things that you need to be aware of:

❁ If you're applying the motif to a piece of clothing such as a child's dress or T-shirt, use a lightweight bonding web – a heavy bonding web will be stiff after it has been fused to the background fabric.

❁ Cut the bonding web slightly smaller than your fabric, so that you don't accidentally fuse the web to your ironing board or to the hot plate of your iron.

❁ Place a clean cloth on top of your motif before you iron it in place to prevent the web from sticking to your iron's hot plate.

❁ If you're worried about your motifs fraying after they have been applied to the background fabric, zigzag stitch or run a thin line of Fray Check – a colourless, liquid sealant that comes with a fine-tipped applicator – around the edges.

Patchwork

I've been making my patchworks for several years, combining vintage fabrics from the 1950s, 60s and 70s with modern printed fabrics. I love the idea that a collection of old fabrics can be sewn together to make something that tells a story, with each square representing a memory. Patchwork is also a fantastic way of making use of old scraps and remnants of fabric that are too small to make into anything else. The ideas shown here are a great way of adding instant colour to a room.

For me, the biggest thrill of patchwork is trying out different fabric and colour combinations until I come up with something that works: it really gives me a buzz! You can read countless books on colour theory and you'll certainly pick up useful tips on what might go with what – but as far as I'm concerned, there is really only one 'rule': if you like it, go for it!

Patchwork throw

Most people who start a patchwork end up quitting before they've finished it, which I think must be soul-destroying! Here's how to make a patchwork the easy way, using a sewing machine. If I had more time, I would love to make a patchwork in the traditional way, sitting by a log burner, sewing each patch by hand – ideally with a sea view! But as a busy mum, I've developed a few simpler methods and the instructions below are very easy.

You will need

Collection of pre-washed fabrics
Sharp scissors
Tape measure
Pencil
Ruler
Square cardboard template
Pins
Needle and contrasting thread
Sewing machine
Iron
Fabric for backing
(possibly an old sheet)

1 Decide how big you'd like each fabric patch to be and cut a square of strong card to that size to use as a template. Here, I opted for a 16-cm (6¼-in.) square template, but I have used larger squares in the past.

2 Using a pencil, draw around your cardboard template on the patterned side of your fabric, so that the line is very visible. Cut out the fabric about 1 cm (⅜ in.) beyond the pencil line. Obviously, the more squares you cut

out, the larger your throw will be. (You don't need to plan the size of your overall throw yet – I normally let it evolve.)

3 Now for the bit I like! Arrange the fabric squares in an order you like the look of. I do this on the floor, so that I can step back and view the patchwork from a distance and all angles. You will also see roughly how large your throw will be and whether or not you need to cut out more pieces.

Save some time...

The larger the fabric squares you use, the quicker your throw will be to make!

4 Once you're happy with the layout, take a photograph and print it out, so that you have a record of the order. (You'll be surprised how easy it is for the pieces to get muddled up!) Gather up the squares for each row of the throw in order, then number the rows.

5 Now you need to pin each row of squares together to form a long horizontal strip. Press under the left-hand edge of each square along the pencil line and pin it along the right-

hand edge of the adjoining square, as shown (hence the importance of having visible pencil lines!).

6 When you've pinned one row, take the strip to your sewing machine and sew, stitching as close to the folded edge of each square as possible, removing the pins as you go. Assemble all the horizontal strips in the same way.

7 Fold under the long bottom edge of each strip along the pencil line and

press. Now pin each strip along the top of the row below, along the pencil line, and stitch as in step 6. Sew strips of fabric together until your throw is the desired size.

8 Cut a piece of backing fabric or an old cotton sheet about 2.5 cm (1 in.) larger all around than the patchwork top. Pin the throw right side on top. It's best to do this on the floor, so that you can keep the fabrics as flat as possible.

Why not...
Try making a cushion with four large squares or lots of miniature squares? If you have young children, you could make cot and dolls' blankets in the same way.

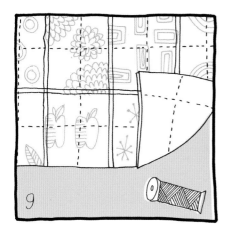

9 Using a needle and thread, tack the front and back panels together along the centre of each strip so you've got horizontal stripes all over your throw. (The stitches will be pulled out, so it doesn't matter if they're unsightly!)

10 Now pin around three edges of your throw (as if making a duvet cover), leaving the bottom edge open. Carefully machine stitch along the three edges, on the reverse of the pencil lines that you drew at the start.

11 Trim off the excess backing fabric, then turn the throw right side out.

12 Press the throw well all over. Turn under the raw open edge along the bottom of the throw along the pencil line, then machine or hand stitch the final edge.

13 For some reason, this last process is the one I like best: using a contrasting thread to make it a feature, hand stitch around all four edges, keeping a neat

but not particularly small running stitch. (I think it's quite alright to see this stitching.) This will prevent the top and bottom panels from sliding around. When you've finished, remove the tacking stitches from step 9.

Now you have your finished throw! You might like to add a personal touch by embroidering the date and possibly a message under one corner for posterity!

Strip patchwork

Making a patchwork is a bit like creating a large picture or collage; the part of the process that I most enjoy is choosing the different fabric combinations. This patchwork, used here as a curtain, is simply made up of strips of fabric stitched together. I've built the design around a deep, colourful central panel of children with balloons and kites, with narrower strips above and below; spend plenty of time playing around with strips of different colours and patterns until you have something that you feel works.

You will need

Colourful fabrics – around ten pieces of varying depths, each 100 cm (40 in.) in length
Fabric for border (optional)
Backing fabric
Pencil
Long ruler
Set square
Scissors
Pins
Tape measure
Iron
Sewing machine

1 Decide how long you want your patchwork to be and make sure you have enough strips to make this length; you will have to turn under the top and bottom edges of each strip by 1 cm (³⁄₈ in.), so remember to take this into account. Decide how wide you'd like your patchwork to be and then cut your fabric strips to the same length plus 2 cm (¾ in.).

2 Lay the strips on the floor and move them around until you have a colour arrangement that you like. I almost always choose fabrics that include a stripe or an obvious pattern; this makes stitching them together easier because there is a visual line to follow. I then take a photo of the layout so that I can refer to it throughout the process as my guide.

Recycle and re-use...

The most challenging part of making a strip patchwork of different fabrics is sourcing pieces that are long enough. Old curtains work very well, especially if parts are worn, as you won't feel too bad about cutting them up!

3 Hand wash all the strips of fabric to avoid any possible shrinkage. When they are dry, press the strips.

4 Take your main fabric panel (in this case, the children with the balloons) and draw a faint pencil line all the way around it, using a set square to ensure that the corners are precise right angles so that you're left with a perfect rectangle.

5 Turn under one long edge of all the remaining strips to the wrong side by

1 cm (³/₈ in.) keeping them straight and using the patterns within the fabric as your guide. Press under the bottom edge of all the strips that are going to go above the main panel, and the top edge of all the strips that are going to go below the main panel.

6 Pin the first fabric strip below the main panel, pinning it along the pencil line to keep it really straight. Then pin the second strip below the first in the same way, making sure that it is

perfectly straight. (I pin only two panels at a time so that it's easier to sew.)

7 Stitch the panels together, stitching a few millimetres (¹/₈ in. or so) from the edge and removing the pins as you go. I don't bother using matching threads, I just stick to white; I think it adds to the charm when you can see where the thread has been stitched.

8 Add the remaining strips in the same way, checking your reference photo

Why not...
Use your patchwork as a curtain? Simply sew a long panel on the reverse at the top leaving the short ends open so that you can slot a curtain rod or wooden dowel through.

regularly to make sure that the pieces are in the right order.

9 I decided to add a border to this patchwork, but it's fine if you don't want to or haven't got enough time. Again, I made life easier for myself by choosing a fabric with a stripe. This was part of an old duvet cover. Old sheets and duvet covers are great, as they're often wonderfully soft and cosy – and as they've been washed many times, there's no chance of them shrinking.

10 Using a ruler, draw a faint pencil line all around the patchwork. Measure the length of the top and cut two border strips to this length and whatever width you want plus 2 cm (¾ in.) Press under one long edge of each strip by 1 cm (⅜ in.) and pin to each side of the patchwork, along the drawn line. Stitch in place.

11 Now measure the width of the top and cut two strips to this length and the same width as the side borders. Press, pin and stitch them in place. Press the whole patchwork.

12 Cut a piece of backing fabric or an old cotton sheet about 2.5 cm (1 in.) larger all around than the top. (I used more of the white duvet fabric that I had used for the borders.) Lay the backing fabric flat; it's best to do this on the floor, so that you can keep the fabrics as flat as possible. Pin the patchwork right side down on top, working from the centre outwards, then tack from the centre of the

top edge down to the centre of the bottom edge, and from the centre of one side edge to the centre of the other side. Again, draw a straight pencil line all around. Taking a 1-cm (⅜-in.) seam, stitch around the top and sides, leaving the bottom open.

13 Turn the patchwork right side out and press flat. Sew around the stitched sides 1 cm (⅜ in.) in from the edge to help the patchwork keep its shape. Fold the raw edges of the bottom of the patchwork in by 1 cm (⅜ in.) and press. Pin, then topstitch along the bottom edge.

Your patchwork is now finished!

2

Printing Fabric

The joys of printing

I was first introduced to screen printing at school when I was a teenager and I remember thinking it was the coolest, cleverest thing ever! My art teacher, Mrs Bruce, was also the coolest ever – she was a total inspiration and I loved everything about her. She was an eccentric: she had black backcombed hair, dark kohl eyeliner, red lips (think Elizabeth Taylor as Cleopatra!) and wore mostly black – which appealed to me, as I did, too!

Since that time, I've experimented with various methods of printing on fabric, some of which are demonstrated in the pages that follow. I've devised designs based on simple cut-out shapes that I can screen print at home, using inexpensive equipment; I've also discovered how to get my own illustrations printed digitally onto fabric and turn them into unique, one-off pieces that are really special to me and my family. To this day, I still get a thrill when peeling back the screen to reveal the first print of an image on fabric. I hope that the ideas shown here will inspire and encourage you to have a go at this creative and utterly absorbing craft.

Printing from masking-tape and paper stencils

The projects shown here use one of the simplest ways of printing your own fabric and are a great introduction to the wonderful world of screen printing. This is what first got me hooked on printing!

You don't need to be a great artist to screen print, but you should try to develop an eye for pattern and colour. Strong, bold shapes and lines work best and can have great impact, even on a relatively small scale. In the projects shown here, I've used only one colour other than the actual colour of the fabric – but as you gain experience and confidence, you can start to introduce other colours and build up designs of increasing complexity.

Here's how!

When I did my first ever screen printing at school, we only had the option of using masking tape or paper stencils. Now there are many more options, including self-adhesive stencils. However, the general principle is the same for all: you position a stencil on the silk screen, which acts as a barrier to the ink – the ink will only go through those parts of the screen that are not covered by the stencil, while the areas where you stick the stencils will remain uncoloured.

You will need

Apron

Old newspaper

Pencil

Masking tape, paper or self-adhesive stencil sheets

Sharp scissors

White cotton or linen fabric cut slightly larger than your screen

Large piece of mountboard or cardboard

Blank silk screen suitable for printing fabric

Brown parcel tape (optional)

Old spoon

Water-based textile inks

Spare pair of hands (an adult ideally!)

Squeegee

Soft sponge

Old tea towel

Hair dryer

Iron

Use a spare car Squeegee

Practice makes perfect...

Screen printing is not an exact science and it's often
Sometimes you need several pulls of the squeegee; sometimes you need to
add a bit of water to make the ink slightly thinner, and sometimes even the
weather and humidity can affect the process.

1 Put on an apron to protect your clothes, then protect your work surface with sheets of old newspaper. Draw the shapes for your design on your chosen stencil material, then cut out the shapes.

2 Take the fabric on which you're going to be printing and lay it on a large piece of mountboard or strong cardboard.

3 If you're using masking tape or self-adhesive stencil sheets, turn your silk screen over so that the mesh isn't touching the table and begin to lay your shapes on it (you'll need to peel off the backing paper from self-adhesive stencil sheets). If you're using paper stencils, place them directly on the fabric you're going to print on; once the screen has been placed on top of the fabric, the paper stencils will stick to the screen for printing.

4 If you'd like a straight edge to your print, use brown parcel tape to mask out four straight edges and frame your design, as shown.

5 Now you're ready for the exciting bit – the printing! Place the screen on top of the fabric, with the mesh touching the fabric. Carefully spoon some ink along the top edge.

Watch and learn...

There are plenty of videos on YouTube showing this process and the angle at which you need to hold the squeegee. If the colour is a bit patchy in areas, gently drag the ink up to the top of the screen (this is called 'flooding' the screen) and repeat the process a few times on a new piece of fabric.

6 If you don't have hinged clamps for your screen, get someone to help you with this bit. Ask your helper to hold the screen down firmly on two sides, while you carefully drag the ink from the top of the screen to the bottom using your squeegee. Repeat, pulling the ink in the same direction – that is, from top to bottom again.

7 Carefully lift the screen off. You should now see your first image printed onto the fabric!

8 If you want to print another piece of fabric, turn your screen around so that you can pull the ink in the opposite direction. This process can be a case of trial and error – you might find that one pull of the squeegee produces a crisp, bold print on your fabric, or you may find that two or three pulls work better.

9 Pull off the stencils and tape. Any excess ink can be scooped back into the pot. Wash your screen with a soft sponge, so that all traces of ink are

removed, then gently rub it as dry as you can with an old tea towel before completing the drying with a hair dryer.

10 Leave your printed panels of fabric to dry completely. You may like to print over the top of your first fabric pieces to produce a two-colour random design.

11 Place a piece of cotton fabric over the printed panels, then press with a hot iron to fix the colour. Alternatively, place in a tumble dryer for 40 minutes.

Summer bunting

This project uses fabric that has been screen printed using masking tape to create crisp, clean, geometric lines. I used bright colours – red, yellow and a luscious apple green – to make vibrant, summery-looking bunting that is just perfect for a garden party or barbecue. With this project, you needn't be too precise with your printing – you only need small pieces of fabric to make bunting, so any colourful pieces of printed fabric can be used.

You will need

Apron
Old newspaper
Masking tape
Template on page 102 (optional)
Sharp scissors
White cotton or linen fabric cut slightly larger than your screen
Large piece of mountboard or cardboard
Blank silk screen suitable for printing fabric
Old spoon
Water-based textile inks
Squeegee
Soft sponge
Old tea towel
Hair dryer
Iron
Pencil and ruler
Pins
Sewing machine and matching thread
White or coloured bias binding

Why not...
Turn some of your panels into cushion covers?
Or, sew squares together to make a tablecloth to
match your bunting — great for a party!

1 Place the silk screen on a flat surface, mesh side up, and stick on strips of masking tape in whatever pattern takes your fancy. Following the instructions on pages 60–63, turn the silk screen over and print your design onto white cotton or linen fabric. Print several pieces in different colours and leave to dry.

2 Press the panels with a hot iron or tumble dry to fix the colour (see page 62). Clean your screen.

3 Cut out a triangular card template. It's entirely up to you what size you make it, but obviously you'll get more from your fabric if it's on the smaller side! Carefully draw around your template on the fabrics and neatly cut out the triangles.

4 Sort your bunting pieces into pairs and pin print sides together along two edges. Taking a 1-cm (³/₈-in.) seam, machine stitch along the two edges of each pair, then trim the seam allowance.

5 Turn the triangles right side out and use a pencil to push out the tips of the triangles into a sharp point. Press under a cotton handkerchief, so that the ink doesn't ruin your iron.

6 Arrange the triangles in an order you like, spacing them roughly 15 cm (6 in.) apart, then pin a strip of folded bias binding over the top edges, leaving at least 15 cm (6 in.) of binding at each end for hanging. Machine stitch along the bias binding and press once more.

Sunshine and showers

The weather where I live is very changeable, so I decided to represent this by printing panels of clouds, sunshine and rain motifs to make a set of colourful cushions. I wanted to create an instant blast of colour that would transform our decking into a happy, vibrant area. You can either use different panels for the fronts and backs of the cushions, so that you can turn them over for different 'weather', or keep the backs as plain fabric.

You will need

Apron

Old newspaper

Pencil

Newsprint paper (available from art shops) or office printing paper

Templates on pages 103–105 (optional)

Sharp scissors

White cotton or linen fabric cut slightly larger than your screen

Large piece of mountboard or cardboard

Blank silk screen suitable for fabric printing

Old spoon

Water-based textile inks

Spare pair of hands (an adult ideally!)

Squeegee

Soft sponge

Old tea towel

Hair dryer

Pros and cons of paper stencils...

With paper stencils you just print, peel off the paper and clean the screen. The disadvantage is that you can't print many prints before the paper creases, peels off and starts to get worn around the edges!

You will need (continued)

Iron

Pins

Sewing machine

Needle and matching thread

Zip (optional)

Cushion pad

Why not...
Try making a
patchwork
tablecloth to match
your cushions?

1 Draw some simple cloud shapes on newsprint or office printing paper and cut them out. Place them on the fabric and arrange them in a loose pattern. When you're happy with your arrangement, gently lower the silk screen onto the design, with the mesh side touching the fabric; don't worry if some of the clouds are off the edge.

2 Following the instructions on pages 60–63, print your design onto the fabric. The act of pulling the ink down the screen will ensure that the cloud stencils stick in place.

3 Repeat steps 1 to 2 to create more cloud panels, as well as panels of sun and rain motifs, then leave them to dry.

Why not... try making co-ordinating napkins or placemats for colourful table settings if you don't want to make something as ambitious as a tablecloth?

4 Press the panels with a hot iron or tumble dry to fix the colour (see page 62). Clean your screen.

5 Decide what size cushion you're able to get from your printed fabric panels and cut a square of cardboard to the size you've chosen plus 1 cm (³⁄₈ in.) all around to allow for the seams. Now draw around your cardboard template of the back of the fabric and cut out two squares for each cushion.

6 Place a pair of panels together, with the printed sides facing inwards, and pin along the sides and bottom. Machine stitch approximately 1 cm (³⁄₈ in.) from the outer edge, starting and stopping 1 cm (³⁄₈ in.) from the top of each side.

7 Turn the cushion cover right side out and press. Fold the raw, unstitched edge to the wrong side by about 5 mm (¼ in.) twice and press. Add your cushion pad and carefully slipstitch along the gap. (If you intend to wash your cover, you might like to sew a zip along the edge instead.)

Wall tidy

My inspiration for this wall tidy came from a childhood memory of my dad's workspace in his garage. He hung a large panel of painted white wood above his workbench and painted on the silhouettes of his tools in turquoise paint, before adding the hooks and fastenings to hold them. It was incredibly neat-looking – and I always thought the board itself looked great, even without the tools!

You will need

Apron
Old newspaper
Plain paper, pencil and tracing paper
Templates on page 106 (optional)
Sticky stencil sheets (available online) or plastic sheets for covering books (available in a roll from stationery shops)
Cutting mat
Craft knife or small utility knife
Large piece of mountboard or cardboard
White linen or cotton fabric cut slightly larger than your screen
Blank silk screen suitable for fabric printing
Brown parcel tape (optional)
Old spoon
Water-based textile inks
Spare pair of hands (an adult ideally!)

Squeegee
Soft sponge
Old tea towel
Hair dryer
Iron
Sharp scissors
Ruler
Plain strong cotton tea towel
Sewing machine
Two wooden batons

Why not...
Print this design onto a ready-made shopping bag or tea towel?

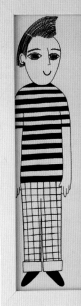

Take care...

Tape the tracing paper and stencil sheet together along a couple of edges, so that they don't slip out of position.

1 Choose objects that you think would look interesting in silhouette form and draw the outlines on plain paper, or trace the templates on page 106.

2 Trace the outlines onto tracing paper, then turn the tracing paper over. Place on scrap paper and scribble over all the pencil lines. Turn the tracing paper over and place it on your adhesive stencil sheet. Now draw over the shapes again, pressing firmly to transfer the lines onto the adhesive sheet.

3 Place the stencil sheet on a cutting mat and carefully cut out your objects with a craft knife or a small, sharp pair of scissors. If you've drawn a pair of spectacles, remember to keep the two lens pieces, as shown.

4 Gently peel the back off your stencil and stick it to the underside of the silk screen. If you've drawn a pair of spectacles, re-position the two cut-out lens pieces, so that they will appear white in the finished piece. For

a straight edge to your print, mask the edges with brown parcel tape.

5 Following the instructions on pages 60–63, print your design onto white cotton or linen. Press the panels with a hot iron or tumble dry to fix the colour (see page 62). Clean your screen.

6 Place a plain white tea towel on your table. Lay the printed panels on top to work out where the different pockets will go. You may want to cut sections

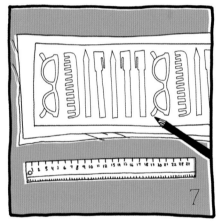

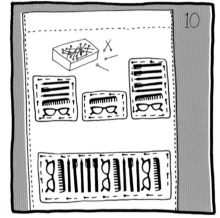

out of your printed panels to make pockets in different sizes.

7 Now back each pocket. Place the fabric print side down on plain cotton fabric and, using a ruler and pencil and leaving at least 1 cm (³/₈ in.) all around the motifs you are going to use, draw all around it to make a rectangle.

8 Pin the layers together. Taking a 1-cm (³/₈-in.) seam, machine stitch around the sides and base along the

pencil line. Trim off the excess fabric.

9 Turn the pockets right side out and press. Fold the raw top edges of each pocket in along the drawn line, then stitch across the top of each pocket.

10 Pin the pockets to the tea towel, leaving 10 cm (4 in.) space top and bottom so that you can make channels for the dowels, and machine stitch around the sides and base of each pocket. If you wish, you can

create sections within the pockets by sewing vertically between the pen motifs. Remove the pins as you go.

11 Turn under the top and bottom edges of the tea towel to the wrong side by 5 cm (2 in.) and machine stitch. Poke a length of wooden baton or dowel through the channels to fix the wall tidy to your wall; alternatively, hammer a nail through each corner. (The batons are used only to prevent the wall tidy from sagging.)

Geometric scarf

I chose a geometric Scandinavian-style pattern in red on white for this project, as I love to wear bright red lipstick and red leather boots and this scarf will always match! Stig Lindberg, one of my all-time favourite Swedish designers from the 1950s and 60s, often used similar patterns to this on his ceramic vases and bowls. Creating a geometric pattern also enables you to continue the pattern in sections to create the long scarf.

You will need

Apron
Old newspaper
Self-adhesive white stencil sheets
Sharp scissors
Pencil (optional)
Large piece of mountboard or cardboard
Plain white cotton or linen fabric cut slightly larger than your screen
Blank silk screen suitable for printing fabric
Brown parcel tape (optional)
Old spoon
Water-based textile ink
Spare pair of hands (an adult ideally!)

Squeegee
Soft sponge
Old tea towel
Hair dryer
Iron
Pins
Sewing machine and matching thread

Why not...
Experiment with a few of the sheets without knowing the outcome! You might have an idea of the types of design you'd like to do for this or you might not. It doesn't really matter – it's fun to see what happens as you start cutting!

1 Take your pair of scissors and one of your stencil sheets and just start cutting! Cut out any shapes that take your fancy – even the simplest of shapes can be effective. If you want to be more precise, you can draw your shapes on the paper side of the stencil sheet first.

2 Turn your silk screen over so that the mesh isn't touching the table and lay your shapes on it. When you're happy with your layout, carefully peel the backing sheet off each piece and

stick it onto the screen. If you'd like a straight edge to your print, use brown parcel tape to mask out four straight edges to frame your design, as shown.

3 Following the instructions on pages 60–63, print your design onto the fabric and leave to dry. Print enough panels to make up the full length of the scarf, with a few spares to be on the safe side. Press with a hot iron or tumble dry for 40 minutes to fix the colour. Clean your screen.

4 Cut your printed panels of fabric into neat rectangles, leaving about 1–2 cm ($^3/_8$–$^3/_4$ in.) unprinted fabric along each long edge of the design. Turn under one short end of each panel and press. Carefully pin the panels together to form a row about 115 cm (45 in.) long, making sure that the printed sections line up with each other.

5 Machine stitch along the turned-under edge of each panel to make a rectangle, removing the pins as you go.

6 Cut a piece of plain fabric the same size as the printed rectangle. Place the printed fabric face down on the plain fabric and pin the two layers together. Taking a 1-cm (³/₈-in.) seam, machine stitch along three sides, leaving one short end unsewn. (You might like to draw a straight pencil line to follow.)

7 Trim the seam allowances, then turn the scarf right side out. Turn the raw edges of the unsewn end under, press and then either slipstitch the unsewn end by hand or topstitch it by machine.

Now you have an eye-catching scarf (or table runner if you aren't feeling brave enough to wear it!).

Geometry time

Varying the size of the triangles and the width of the lines gives the design a feeling of vitality.

If you like symmetry, as I do, make sure that the two halves of the scarf mirror each other. Here, for example, I made sure that I had bands of large triangles at each end of the scarf, so that it would look balanced and symmetrical when worn.

Experiment with other geometric shapes – squares, rectangles, circles, even hexagons – but try not to include too many different shapes in the same design, or it could start to look confusing.

Printing using an exposed screen

With this method, you make stencils of the shapes that you want to be coloured on your fabric rather than the shapes you want to remain white. The printing technique is the same as in the previous chapter – you just need to get your head around the difference between negative and positive images!

All artwork that is going to be exposed onto a screen must be created in black and white; the shapes that you want to print must be black, while the background must be white. This method of printing can produce very bold or incredibly fine detailed lines and is the most versatile method of screen printing, although it is normally favoured by those who have had a taster of screen printing with paper stencils first.

Here's how!

This method is slightly different to using paper stencils to stick onto a screen, as the pieces that you cut out are the shapes that you will actually see printed. There are several companies that will expose the screen and even print the fabric for you; you can find details on page 110.
I recommend that you get a specialist company to expose the screen for you. You can even ask them to print your design onto fabric if you wish – you will need to give them instructions on what colour you'd like them to

You will need

Apron

Old newspaper

Pencil

Masking tape, paper or self-adhesive stencil sheets

Sharp scissors

White cotton or linen fabric cut slightly larger than your screen

Large piece of mountboard or cardboard

Blank silk screen suitable for printing fabric

Brown parcel tape (optional)

Old spoon

Water-based textile inks

Spare pair of hands (an adult ideally!)

Squeegee

Soft sponge

Old tea towel

Hair dryer

Iron

print with, what fabric you want them to print on and the amount of fabric that you want. Companies will often let you see the layout and a sample first. Alternatively, you can use the exposed screen to print the fabric yourself, following the instructions on pages 60–63.

Preparing your design

1 First, you need to create your black-and-white design. The projects that follow set out two different methods of doing this: gluing black paper cut-outs onto white paper, or applying dark-coloured stickers to white paper.

2 If you're gluing down paper cut-outs to make your design, you now need to scan and neaten up the edges, so that the edges of the stuck-down paper can't be seen. If you're lucky enough to have a large scanner/printer at home and are savvy with Photoshop or another image-manipulation program, then you can do this stage yourself. If you are not, get it done at a local photocopier shop or by the company that is going to expose your screen.

3 The next stage is to convert the black-and-white version into a PDF, Tiff or JPEG file to email to the screen-printing company that will be producing the exposed screen for you.

Exposing your design onto the screen

1 The screen-printing company will transfer your design onto a sheet of clear transparency film via a photocopier or computer printer. If you're emailing a company with your design, then they will print it straight from your file onto this transparency sheet.

2 Next, they coat a blank silk screen with light-sensitive photo-emulsion fluid and place it in a darkened room with absolutely no daylight coming in – ideally, a windowless room – to dry. The transparency sheet (with your design on) is then placed over the silk screen and exposed to ultraviolet light. When the screen is washed, the areas of emulsion that were not exposed to light (that is, the black parts of the design) dissolve and wash away, leaving a positive of the image on the screen mesh.

3 The screen is now ready for printing and can be used hundreds of times if it is treated well.

Printing fabric using an exposed screen

To print the fabric yourself, just follow the instructions on pages 60–63; the only difference is that, with an exposed screen, the image won't peel off or wash off!

Christmas stocking

I've always been attracted to Scandinavian Christmas designs, particularly ones in bright red and white, which combine graphic colour combinations with simple folk-art motifs such as hearts. This is what provided the inspiration for this Christmas stocking. You could print similar motifs onto plain white linen napkins for a fully co-ordinated Christmas look! If you're good at sewing, you might like to line your stocking with a contrasting fabric.

You will need

White and black paper
Template on page 107 (optional)
Craft knife
Cutting mat
Glue stick
Printed stocking fabric panel
Plain white linen or cotton fabric
Ruler
Pencil
Scissors
Pins
Iron
Sewing machine

1 Start by drawing a simple Christmas stocking shape on white paper. Now cut strips and circles (or any shape you fancy) of black paper and arrange them on the stocking template.

2 When you are happy with your layout, use a glue stick to carefully glue them onto the template, then cut around the drawn pencil line. Now stick the whole stocking onto a large piece of white paper.

3 Following the instructions on pages 80–81, prepare and print your design (or have it professionally printed) onto fabric.

4 Place your printed stocking fabric panel print side down on a flat surface and draw around the edge with a pencil. This will later become your sewing line.

Why not...
Make things even simpler, and use ribbon for the hanging loop?

Make things easier…

Fold your black paper several times, so that you're cutting through several layers when you cut out your shapes – this way, they'll be the same size.

5 Place the panel print side down on the plain white fabric and pin it in place. Cut a straight line across the top of the stocking as shown, roughly 5 cm (2 in.) from the printed edge.

6 Sew all the way around the stocking on top of the pencil line, leaving the straight, top edge unstitched. Cut out the stocking, cutting about 1 cm (3/8 in.) beyond the pencil line. If you have an overlocker, overlock the edges to prevent fraying. If you do not, zigzag stitch around the edge.

7 Turn the stocking right side out, place some cotton fabric on top, and press. Fold the top edges over twice by about 1 cm (3/8 in.) and press.

8 Cut a strip of plain fabric measuring roughly 12 x 5 cm (5 x 2 in.). Press it in half lengthways, then fold the raw edges in to the centre creaseline and press again. Topstitch along the long unfolded edge. Fold in half and pin to the inside of the stocking, centred over the back seam. Stitch around the top edge of the stocking, close to the folded-over hem.

Stocking fillers

Why not hang lots of stockings in alternating colours along your hallway or up your staircase? A few years ago, I took an order from a man who owned a company on 5th Avenue, New York: he bought 50 of my stockings – 25 red and 25 blue – to give to his employees for Christmas. On the last working day, he hung the stockings on his staff's coat hooks down a long corridor, alternating the colours, and filled them with candy!

Other motifs that would work well for this project could include:

✿ A simple Christmas-tree motif

✿ Your child's name

✿ White stars on a blue background

✿ A stylized reindeer head with antlers

Alternatively, why not make a big drawstring sack printed with Christmassy motifs and leave it by your child's bed on Christmas Eve, so that Santa can fill it with presents?

Table runner

My inspiration for this design came from making sticker pictures with my four-year-old daughter one Sunday morning. I bought a packet containing sheets of stickers in various shapes and we both played with them, creating designs on paper. For this project, you need to pay someone to expose the screen for you to print at home (see pages 80–81).

You will need

Sticker shapes
White paper
Soft pencil and ruler (optional)
Access to a scanner or photocopier
Apron
Old newspaper
Large piece of mountboard or cardboard
Blank silk screen suitable for printing fabric
Water-based textile ink
Old spoon
Spare pair of hands (an adult ideally!)
Squeegee
Soft sponge
Old tea towel
Hair dryer
Iron
Pins
White cotton fabric
Sewing machine

1 Keeping to one colour, start sticking your stickers onto a piece of paper in your chosen pattern. As you're designing the print for a table runner, you might like to draw a very faint rectangle on the paper to help keep the design straight. You may need to make several attempts before you come up with a version you're happy with.

2 If you have access to a scanner and can work in Photoshop or another image-manipulation program, scan your design and convert all the coloured stickers to black. If you can't do this at home, any good photocopying centre will be able to do this for you. Then convert the black-and-white version into a PDF, Tiff or JPEG file and email it to the screen-printing company that is producing the exposed screen for you (see pages 80–81).

Why not...

Make matching napkins?
Print your pattern onto
square panels of fabric and
hem them in the same way
as the table runner

Why not...
Try printing tea towels and napkins in a variety of different colours?

3 Once you've received your exposed screen, print several pieces of white cotton following the instructions on pages 60–63, leaving a generous white border all around the pattern.

4 Turn under one short end of each panel and press. Carefully pin the panels together to form a row, making sure that the printed sections line up with each other.

5 Machine stitch along the turned-under edge of each panel, removing the pins as you go.

6 Turn the raw edges to the wrong side by 1 cm (³⁄₈ in.) twice and press.

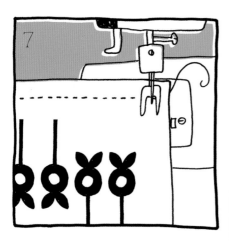

7 Machine stitch all around the table runner to form a neat hem.

Take the heat off

Table runners seem to be very common in Scandinavian countries, but less so in the UK. I rather like them, as they add a bit of colour to the table and you can use them without having to use a tablecloth. You can also place salad bowls on them without having to use lots of placemats – and they're easier and quicker to wash than a large tablecloth!

To stop hot dishes from leaving a nasty white mark on your table top, here's how to make a heat-resistant version. After step 5, measure your table runner and cut a piece of heat-resistant wadding (available online and from good patchwork and quilting shops) and a piece of backing fabric to the same size. Place the wadding on your work surface, with the table runner right side up on top, and tack them together. Place the backing fabric right side down on top of that. Pin and tack the three layers together, then machine stitch around three sides, leaving one short end unstitched. Turn right side out through the unstitched end and press. Turn the raw edges of the short side under and slipstitch in place. Remove the tacking stitches.

If you wish, topstitch around all four sides in a contrasting colour of thread for a decorative finishing touch.

Digitally printed fabric

Recent advancements in technology mean that it's now possible for anyone to get their designs printed onto fabric – so you can create unique, one-off pieces for your home. Here are some simple ideas to get you started.

As long as you're able to scan a design into a computer and make a file of it, the way you create your design is completely up to you. Fabric can be digitally printed from a photo, collage, fabric picture, pen-and-ink drawing, embroidery, pencil sketch, watercolour painting – the sky's the limit! It's a wonderful moment when your parcel arrives through the letterbox and you see your design printed on fabric!

Here's how!

All the online companies that offer this service let you know in detail what they need from you, but here are the basic steps to getting a design digitally printed.

Fabric-printing companies

I've used two companies to digitally print the fabric used in this section: the Centre for Advanced Textiles (www.catdigital.co.uk) in Glasgow, and Spoonflower (www.spoonflower.com).

The Centre for Advanced Textiles is more expensive but offers a superb service and it's possible to speak to an advisor over the phone. They're responsible for reprinting some of Britain's most famous fabrics, such as those designed by Lucienne Day.

1 Produce a piece of artwork, design or pattern that you wish to be replicated onto fabric.

2 Scan your design into a computer and make a file of it.

3 Log on to the website of the company you've chosen to digitally print your fabric and upload your file in the format they require.

4 Within the website, you'll now have the chance to review your design and to play around with the size, change the colours (if you like), create a repeated pattern and so on. You'll be able to choose what type of fabric you'd like your design to be printed on and the length of fabric you'd like to order. You then pay for your fabric, which should be printed and posted within a few weeks.

Lavender bags

The digital fabric used in this project was created from some of my daughter's coloured pencil drawings and a few sketches of my own. I cut out all the individual pieces of artwork, placed them on a large piece of paper and glued them down, leaving plenty of space between the motifs. It didn't particularly matter how they looked en masse, as I knew they were going to be cut up! This is such a fun and easy project – perfect for creating little gifts for the relatives at Christmas!

You will need

Your digitally printed fabric
Plain fabric for backing
Sharp scissors
Pencil
Ruler
Pins
Sewing machine
Small bag of dried lavender
Needle and matching thread

Why not...
Use some of your leftover fabric to cover some more matchboxes with matching lavender bags inside (see page 18)?

1 Begin by cutting out individual pictures from your printed fabric, keeping as much border around them as possible. Our designs suited rectangular shapes, but you could do circles, hearts or any other shape you wish.

2 Place the panels face down on some backing fabric, draw a straight pencil line around all four sides, and pin together.

3 Machine stitch along the three pencil lines (or backstitch by hand if you don't have a machine), then trim off the excess fabric.

4 Turn each bag right side out and press. Fold the unsewn edges in along the pencil line and press.

5 Fill your little bags with lavender (making a paper funnel will make this easier). Finally, slipstitch the unsewn edge.

Now you have your cute little lavender bags!

Floral cushion

I chose a 1960s-style flower motif for this cushion, as flowers are what I enjoy drawing most and feature on a large proportion of the fabrics I collect. Throughout the 1960s and 70s, bold flower prints were hugely popular for curtains; I decided to have my design printed in black and white to give it a more contemporary feel.

You will need

Your digitally printed fabric

Templates on pages 108–109 (optional)

Sharp scissors

Tape measure

Pins

Pencil

Ruler

Set square

Sewing machine and matching thread

35-cm (14-in.) cushion pad

Black and white...

I drew a simple four-flower design on a piece of red paper, cut it out and stuck it onto white paper. I then scanned it into the computer, turned the red into black (in Photoshop) and uploaded the file to www.spoonflower.com to be printed on fine cotton fabric.

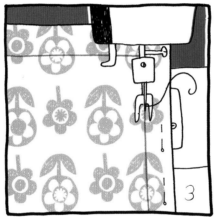

1 Cut two 38-cm (15-in.) squares from your printed fabric and press them flat.

2 Pin the squares printed sides together. Draw a 35-cm (14-in.) square on the top panel, using a set square to ensure that the corners are at perfect right angles.

3 Stitching along the pencil line, machine stitch around three sides, removing the pins as you go.

4 If you have an overlocker, use it to overlock the edges. If you do not, trim off the excess fabric and zigzag stitch the edges.

5 Turn the cushion cover right side out. Turn the unsewn edge in along the pencil line and press.

6 Insert your cushion pad and pin the open two ends together. Now sew along the final edge with a sewing machine or slipstitch by hand.

Why not...

Use your digitally printed fabric to make a tea towel and fabric-covered storage jars (see page 20) for the kitchen, or scatter cushions and herbal sachets for the bedroom?

Design tips

The digitally printed fabric on the opposite page exemplifies some of the design principles that I use every day in my work. These are not hard-and-fast 'rules', but you might find them useful!

✿ Keep it simple! I often use only two colours in my fabric designs – the colour of the fabric itself and one other. Make sure there's a strong contrast: red and white is on of my favourite combinations. Analogous colours (colours that are close together on the traditional artist's colour wheel, such as or blue and green) do not have as much impact.

✿ Once you've decided on your basic motif, ring the changes a bit. Here, I reversed the colours in alternate flowers – red flower on white, then white flower on red. To break things up even more, I also had two variations on the red flower. One has a large white circle in the centre of the flower head. The other has a solid red flower head with four white dots inside it, angled to give the design more movement and make it more dynamic. I also gave one of the red flowers two pairs of leaves.

I've had so much fun putting together the projects for this book. It's given me the chance to revisit some of my favourite fabrics and come up with new ones – the dream job for any textile designer! I hope you've enjoyed the journey, too. Check out the blog on my website (www.janefoster. co.uk) to see what I get up to next – and let me know what you think of my work!

Jane
foster

Templates

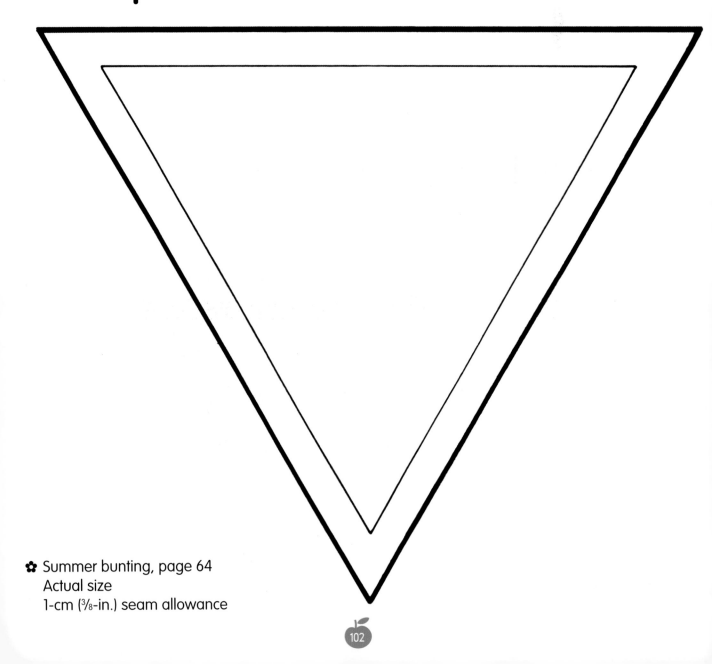

❁ Summer bunting, page 64
Actual size
1-cm (⅜-in.) seam allowance

✿ Sunshine and showers, page 66
Rain clouds
Enlarge by 200%

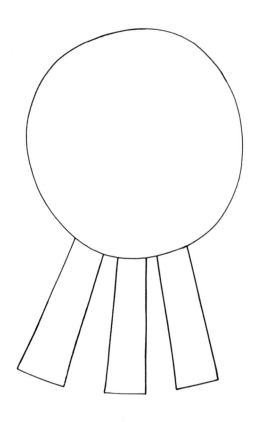

✿ Sunshine and showers, page 66
Sun
Enlarge by 200%

✿ Sunshine and showers, page 66
Tree
Enlarge by 200%

✿ Wall tidy, page 70
Pens
Actual size

✿ Wall tidy, page 70
Pens
Actual size

✿ Christmas stocking, page 92
Enlarge by 200%

✿ Floral cushion, page 96
   Scan and resize as required (see page 92)

Suppliers

Websites for vintage fabric

Donna Flower
(www.donnaflower.com)
eBay (www.ebay.co.uk)
Etsy (www.etsy.com)
Pineapple Retro
(www.pineappleretro.co.uk)
Pomme de Jour
(www.etsy.com/uk/shop/
Pommedejour)
Something Fine
(www.somethingfine.co.uk)

Websites selling Scandinavian fabric

Hus & Hem (www.husandhem.co.uk)
Ikea (www.ikea.com)
Scandinavian Design Centre
(www.scandiaviandesigncenter.com)
Skandium (www.skandium.com)
The Swedish Fabric Company
(www.theswedishfabriccompany.com)

Websites for vintage/ retro-style fabric and basic sewing equipment

By Graziela (www.bygraziela.com)
Contemporary Cloth
(www.contemporarycloth.com)
Ditto Fabrics (www.dittofabrics.co.uk)
Fabric Rehab
(www.fabricrehab.co.uk)
Fabric Worm (www.fabricworm.com)
Merrick and Day
(www.merrick-day.com)

Websites for screen-printing supplies

Art 2 Screen (www.art2screen.co.uk)
Handprinted (www.handprinted.net)
London Graphics
(www.londongraphics.co.uk)
Screen Stretch
(www.screenstretch.co.uk)
Wicked Printing Stuff
(www.wickedprintingstuff.com)

Screen-printing courses

Here are a few I can recommend –
there are lots more around the UK.
Glasgow Print Studio
(www.gpsart.co.uk)
Ink Spot Press (Brighton)
(www.inkspotpress.co.uk) – this is
where I used to print!
Print Club London (www.
printclublondon.com/workshops)
Print Course (www.printcourse.co.uk)

Digital printing

These online companies will digitally
print your designs onto fabric.
Be Fab (www.BeFabBeCreative.co.uk)
Centre for Advanced Textiles (CAT)
(www.catdigital.co.uk)
The Clever Baggers
(www.thecleverbaggers.co.uk)

Companies who can screen-print your designs

Centre For Advanced Textiles (CAT)
(www.catdigital.co.uk)
The Clever Baggers
(www.thecleverbaggers.co.uk)
Countryside Art
(www.countrysideart.co.uk)

Acknowledgements

Many thanks to:

My partner Jim and daughter Polly for all their continuous love,
encouragement and support.
My agent, Claudia Webb, for giving me this wonderful opportunity and being
such a kind and patient person to work with.
The super team at Collins & Brown.
My good friend Alun Callender who took the wonderful photos for this book.
Kate Sutton for coming on board to provide the wonderful illustrations.

Index

Ashley, Laura 6

bags 70
bonding web, fusible 43
boxes 18–19, 31, 95
bunting, Summer 64, 102

Centre for Advanced Textiles, Glasgow 15, 92
Christmas stocking 82–5, 107
colour 99
curtains 52, 53
cushions 26, 98
   floral 96–7, 108–9
   patchwork 49
   screen-printed 65
   sunshine and showers 66–9, 103–4

Day, Lucienne 13, 15, 92

fading 39
Figgjo Flint 6
floral fabric 40–2, 96–7, 108–9
frames 34, 38–9

Groag, Jacqueline 13, 15, 36
Gustavsberg 6

Habitat 6
Hall, Peter 13
Heals 6

Isola, Maija 13

Kandinsky, Wassily 13
Klee, Paul 13

lampshade 22–5
lavender bags 94–5
Lindberg, Stig 6, 74

Mahler, Marian 13, 15, 36
Marimekko 6
Markelius, Sven 36
Miró, Joan 13
motifs 31, 40–2, 85, 99, 107

napkins 68, 87, 88, 103–4

Parsons, David 13
patchwork 44–53
patterns 31, 64, 74–7
pictures, fabric 34–43
pots 20–1
printing fabric 56–99
   digitally 90–9
   printing from masking tape and stencils 58–77
   using an exposed screen 78–89
prints 31
'Pythagoras' 36

retro fabrics 12–53
Riley, Bridget 13
Rörstrand 6
runner, table 86–9

Sanderson 6, 15
scarf, geometric 74–7
screen printing 56–99
silk 39
squeegee 61, 62
stocking, Christmas 82–5, 107

stools 28–30
storage jars 20–1, 98
sun damage 39
sunshine and showers 66–9, 103–4

table runner 86–9
tablecloths 67, 103–4
tea towels 32–3, 70, 88, 98
templates 102–9

UV protection 39

vintage fabrics 12–53

wall tidy 70–3, 105–6
Westman, Marianne 6
White, Mary 13

BOOKS FOR BUSY HANDS
COLLINS & BROWN
WWW.LOVECRAFTS.CO.UK

Join our crafting community at LoveCrafts – we look forward to meeting you!